THE ALPHABET BOOK OF
BREATHING
FOR CHILDREN

Marj Murray
Audrey Redmond
Illustrations by Brian van Wyk

Portal Works

**THIS BOOK IS DEDICATED TO
HARRY AND MAUREEN MURRAY
& JONTY AND SABI REDMOND**

ACKNOWLEDGEMENTS

We would like to acknowledge family and friends who believed in this fun and important project and encouraged us to get the book finished. To the Breathwork Africa and wider breathwork community who continue to support our passion for sharing conscious breathing far and wide.

Deep gratitude to Dr Ela Manga, who brings the breath alive every day and is a constant source of inspiration.

To breath itself – without it we wouldn't be here – and neither would this book.

www.breathworkafrica.co.za
www.breathcafe.com
info@breathworkafrica.co.za

Published by Portal Works
Johannesburg, South Africa

First edition 2022
Copyright ©breathworkafrica2022

All rights reserved. No part of this publication may be reproduced, stored in a retrieval system or transmitted in any form or by any means, electronic, mechanical, photocopying, recording or otherwise, without the prior written permission of the copyright owners.

Cover design	Brian van Wyk
Typesetting	Lindie Metz
Illustrations	Brian van Wyk
ISBN	978-0-6397-1617-6

Disclaimer: The techniques in this book are to support a child through daily challenges and is not a diagnostic tool for any health issues. A doctor's advice should be sought if anyone is experiencing breathing difficulties.

CONTENTS

FOREWORD	6	NUMBERS BREATHING	38
INTRODUCTION	8	OCEAN BREATH	40
ASKING BREATH	12	PALM BREATH	42
BUNNY BREATH	14	QUICK BREATH	44
CALMING BREATH	16	RAINBOW BREATH	46
DOLPHIN BREATH	18	SNAKE BREATH	48
EARTH BREATH	20	TAKE 5 BREATH	50
FLOWER BREATH	22	UMOYA BREATH	52
GIRAFFE BREATH	24	VUVUZELA BREATH	54
HUMMING BEE BREATH	26	WARRIOR BREATH	56
INSECT BREATH	28	LETTER X	58
JABULANI BREATH	30	YAWNING	60
KINDNESS BREATH	32	ZEBRA BREATH	62
LION'S BREATH	34	QUICK GUIDE	64
MY BREATH	36	THE CONTRIBUTORS	66

FOREWORD

A recent longitudinal study involving more than 1000 children found that 98% of 4 year olds tested at creative genius level which surprisingly dropped to 12% in 10 years. As we develop and our brains are shaped by what we are exposed to, what we learn and experience, creative potential remains underneath the layers of societal conditioning and systems that place emphasis on a specific kind of learning. Research in the field of neuroscience and breathing suggests that disconnection from our creative potential corresponds to the disruption of breathing patterns which become more restricted and inflexible as they are impacted by modern living.

Conscious breathing is an unrecognised yet crucial aspect of both our education and healthcare systems. Now more than ever we have a profound responsibility to our children, the future generation, to support their connection to their innate capacity for creativity and emotional intelligence throughout the developmental years and in all aspects of learning, especially through our technology driven lifestyle.

In this fun, joyful and empowering guide to conscious breathing for the 21st century child, Marj Murray and Audrey Redmond bring creative joy and cognitive learning together through memorable curious characters and fun breathing techniques.

Marj and Audrey combine their years of experience in working with children and their expertise in breathwork to bring you this delightful guide to breathing that should be on the bookshelf of every family, school library and community centre.

The simple and universally accessible practices will enchant and support both children and their caregivers to stay connected to creativity, emotional intelligence, growth and learning through breath, the gift of life itself.

May you and all your children learn through this wonderful tool.

Dr Ela Manga

Integrative Medical Doctor
Founder of Breathwork Africa
Johannesburg, July 2022.

INTRODUCTION

Welcome to the A-Z journey of fun and playful Breaths.

This book was inspired by the work of Breathwork Africa and their commitment to share conscious breathing with people of all ages. It is our wish that conversations and joyful interactions are stimulated between children of all ages through the pages of this creation.

Breathing techniques are not another item to add to your 'to do' list, but rather an invitation to weave the fun into your everyday lives.

CONSCIOUS BREATHWORK

Breathing is the easiest tool we can gift our children to help them self-regulate and manage their lives. It is a healthy and effective strategy to build emotional intelligence, self-awareness, and compassionate resilience. It is the ultimate tool to help them stay grounded and access joy.

Conscious breathwork is bringing your attention to your breath and emotion and then consciously modifying the rhythm to influence the way you feel, think, and perceive the world.

Conscious breathing helps children to manage their stressors both at school and at home. It allows them to cope with frustrations of sibling rivalry, anxiety around safety, exam stress, social engagement, and independence. It helps with restful sleep, restoring energy levels, confidence in the classroom and self-esteem, to mention a few.

The younger children are when taught this skill the greater an impact it will have on them later in their lives. Breathwork can change the way people connect with themselves and others and guides the young in coping with the demands of the modern world.

HOW TO USE THIS BOOK: GUIDE TO PARENTS, TEACHERS, AND CHILDREN

The techniques in this book reflect three main self-regulation categories. These include energising, relaxing and balancing the nervous system.

Regulation is the ability to harness more energy when its needed and to dissipate excess energy if required. To allow for a state of balance for focus and concentration that supports learning and memory, and to train relaxation into the body.

In addition, there is an Awareness category. Breath awareness is the foundation of all breathing and mindfulness practices.

By changing the way we breathe intentionally, we are able to navigate to the most appropriate state to support ourselves in the demands of the moment. This intuitive skill is refined through practicing breathwork regularly.

The Alphabet Book of Breathing for Children is a taster of the creative and fun world of breath. For a child to easily find which breathing technique they can use for a specific regulation practice we have added differentiating colours to the page borders which also support the character's personality.

Awareness - all three characters (Coco, Bodhi and Ziggy), the border of the page is purple and yellow
Relaxation - Coco has a blue and orange border
Balance - Bodhi has a green and brown border
Energy - Ziggy has a red and beige border

This will enable children to identify with the colours and characters of this book so that they may find it as a guide to use by themselves.

MEET THE CHARACTERS AND THEIR BREATHING POWERS

We would like to introduce you to the characters of this book. Their unique personalities support the regulation categories described on previous pages.

Ziggy, an energised Meerkat, who uses the breath to invite in energy. Ziggy's techniques can be used if there is a lull in energy levels in the classroom or prior to having to do homework. Using Ziggy's techniques can energise and get you ready for action. Equally, Ziggy's techniques can be used to dissipate excess energy that might make you feel anxious. Ziggy's breathing power is to increase the size of the inhale to build this energy.

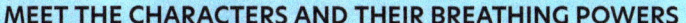

Coco is a Cool Cat! Relaxed and looking at the world from a calm and restful place, Coco believes in rest and relaxation as much as possible. Coco's breathing power is to breathe out slowly.

Bodhi the Bear is feeling balanced, steering between having lots of energy AND feeling too relaxed or even a little lazy. Breathing like Bodhi creates the perfect balance for learning new things and remembering them. Ideal for study and exam time or when needing to focus on something for a period of time. Bodhi's breathing power is that the inhale and exhale are the same length.

Using these breathing powers we encourage you to make up your own breaths, give them names and share them with your friends.

ASKING BREATH

Start at the top of your body and ask your head how it is feeling today. Stop and listen. Take a big breath in and sigh it out.

Then ask your heart how it is feeling. Stop and listen. Take a big breath in and sigh it out.

Lastly, ask your whole body how it is feeling today. Stop and listen. Take a big breath in and sigh it out.

Listen carefully to how your body is feeling today.

BUNNY BREATH

A bunny uses its nose to sniff out delicious carrots that grow in the garden. See if you can find the carrots in this garden and when you do, sniff in three times through your nose and then breathe out through your mouth with an AAAHH sound. Can you do this for all the carrots on the page?

If you are feeling sad and want to cry, you can do the bunny breath to feel better.

Note for adult: This technique mimics crying and helps release big emotions.

CALMING BREATH

Imagine you are visiting a place that makes you happy. Breathe in slowly through your nose while thinking of this happy place. Breathe out slowly through your nose and imagine you are in your happy place.

Can you feel your breath tickling your nose? Can you feel your body relaxing?

Slow your breathing down even more, feel the calmness and safety that this happy place brings.

If you are feeling scared or worried about something, use the Calming Breath.

DOLPHIN BREATH

Imagine dolphins jumping out of water to take a breath in for a count of 3 and when they dive back into the water, they blow the breath out for a count of 3 while making bubbles.

Can you breathe in through your nose for a count of 3 and then breathe out through your mouth for a count of 3.

Have fun pretending you are a dolphin.

EARTH BREATH

Standing barefoot on the grass, feel the grass tickling your feet. Relax your body and imagine you are taking a big breath from the earth.

Bend over and touch the grass with your hands. Imagine breathing the energy from the earth starting at your feet and stretching up bringing your earth breath right to the top of your fingers as you try to touch the sky.

Then bend down again and do the Earth Breath all over again.

Breathe in and out through your nose for the Earth Breath.

If your head is feeling too full of thoughts, then use the Earth Breath.

FLOWER BREATH

Pick a flower or imagine you have one in your hand. Breathe in through your nose as you smell the flower, breathe out slowly through your mouth while gently blowing on the petals of the flower.

Share the smell with nature and with your friends. Let this breath make you smile.

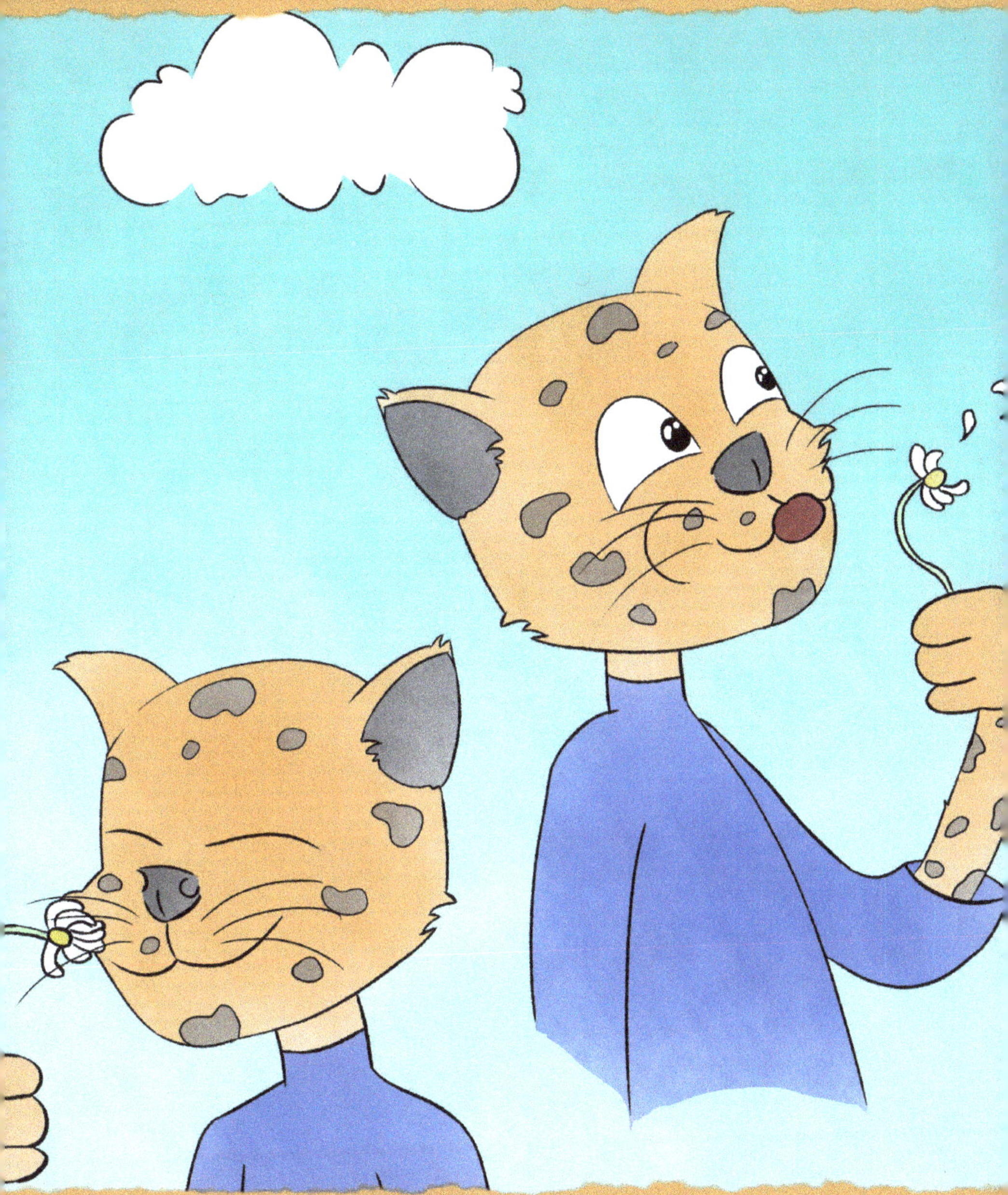

GIRAFFE BREATH

A giraffe has a very long neck. Pretend your arms are the giraffe's neck and as you breathe in through your nose reach to the top branches of a tree.

Stretch, stretch, stretch high up. When you reach the top of the tree, you become thirsty and you bend down with that long neck as you slowly breathe out through your mouth and reach down to the pool of water next to the tree.

Relax your body as you reach down to the water a few times.

HUMMING BEE BREATH

Can you make a humming sound?
Imagine you are a bee humming your favourite
song as you visit all the flowers in the garden.
Breathe in through your nose slowly and hum
your breath out. Pretend you are buzzing
from flower to flower.

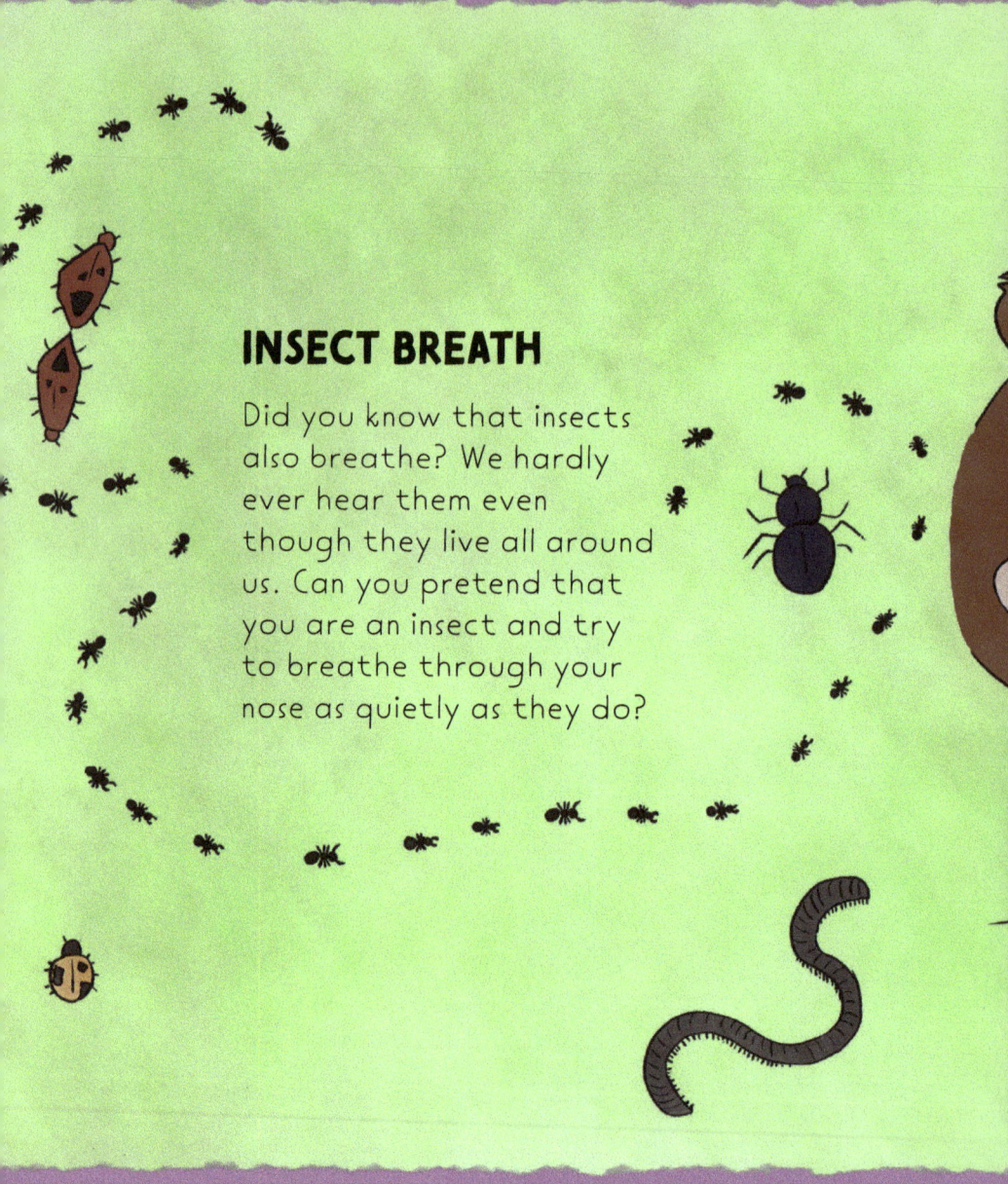

INSECT BREATH

Did you know that insects also breathe? We hardly ever hear them even though they live all around us. Can you pretend that you are an insect and try to breathe through your nose as quietly as they do?

KINDNESS BREATH

Imagine breathing kindness into your heart. Then breathe kindness out of your heart for your family.

Breathing in kindness for yourself, breathing out kindness for your friends.

Breathing in kindness for yourself, breathing out kindness for all the animals, trees, and plants of the world.

Breathing in kindness for yourself, breathing out kindness for everyone in the world.

Do the Kindness Breath through your nose.

LION'S BREATH

Get onto your hands and knees and pretend you are a lion.

Stop, take a big breath in through your mouth and ROAR the breath out loudly through your mouth while making a sound like a lion.

To look even more brave, stick your tongue out while you ROAR.

MY BREATH

Ask yourself if your breathing feels like Ziggy, Bodhi, or Coco's breath today.

Ziggy is full of **ENERGY**.

Bodhi is feeling **FOCUSED**.

Coco is very **RELAXED**.

NUMBERS BREATHING

Let us choose the number 8. Draw a big 8 on a page or in the sand.

Breathe in through your nose as you trace the number 8 with your finger and breathe out through your nose as you complete drawing the number 8.

You can try this with other numbers too while keeping your breaths slow and equal.

OCEAN BREATH

Take a breath in through your nose for a count of 2 as the wave crashes on the beach. Let your breath out through the nose for a count of 2 as the wave flows out to the sea. Do this 3 times.

If you are worried about something, use the Ocean Breath to calm yourself down.

PALM BREATH

Rub the palms of your hands together as fast as you can and feel the heat between your hands.

Gently place your hands over your eyes while you breathe in and out through your nose. Enjoy the feeling of warm hands over your eyes.

Rub your palms together again, place them on your shoulders and make your breath quiet as you breathe in and out through your nose.

Rub your palms together again and place them on your belly, feel your belly grow as you take a breath in through your nose and flatten as you let your breath go.

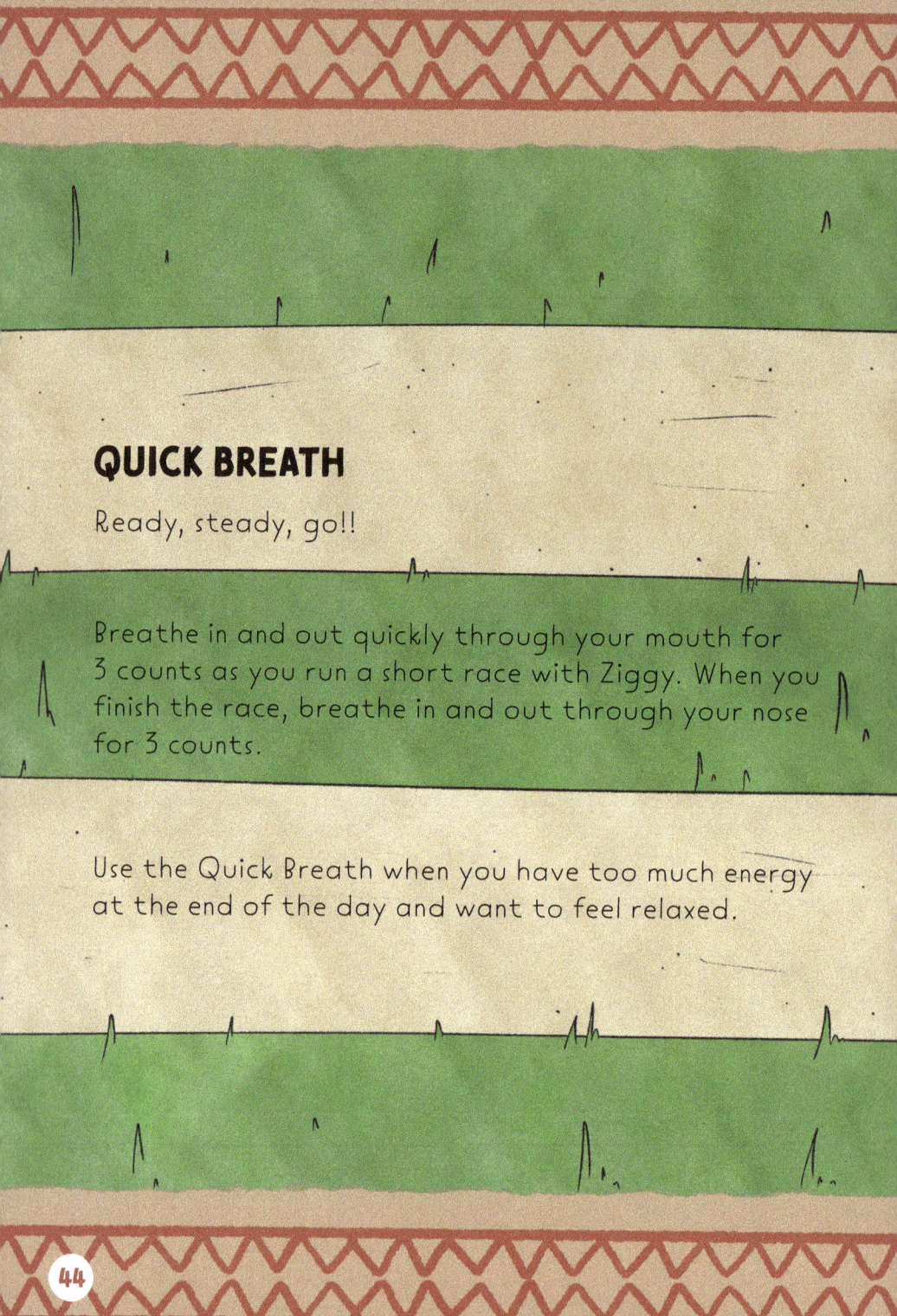

QUICK BREATH

Ready, steady, go!!

Breathe in and out quickly through your mouth for 3 counts as you run a short race with Ziggy. When you finish the race, breathe in and out through your nose for 3 counts.

Use the Quick Breath when you have too much energy at the end of the day and want to feel relaxed.

RAINBOW BREATH

Take a deep breath in through your nose as you raise your arms to the sky. When you breathe out through your mouth, make the shape of a big colourful rainbow with your hands. You can even name your favourite colour as you stretch out your arms.

The Rainbow Breath is great to use when you wake up and want to stretch before you start your day.

TAKE 5 BREATH

We use our hands for this technique. Stretch your one hand out in front of you (as though you're giving someone a high 5) and with the finger from the other hand trace the outline of your fingers on the outstretched hand. Breathing in through your nose as you trace up the finger (up the mountain) and breathing out through your nose as your finger slides down into the valley (between fingers). Complete your whole hand and repeat on the other side.

You can also draw your hand on a piece of paper and trace the outline – breathe in through your nose while going up the side of your finger and breathe out through your nose while going down the side of your finger.

Take 5 can be used anytime during the day or night, when you want to relax or are bored.

UMOYA* BREATH

Coco is breathing in through the nose and breathing a long, slow, relaxing breath out of the mouth.

Coco is making the sound of the wind blowing.

The Umoya Breath can be used when you want to relax your body and your mind and before you go to bed.

*Xhosa word meaning spirit, air, wind.

VUVUZELA* BREATH

This is an instrument often used at football games to celebrate when a goal is scored.

Pretend you have a vuvuzela and take a breath in through your nose and blow a big breath out your mouth while making a big noise.

This is a fun breath.

*a long horn, often made of plastic, blown as part of celebrations.

LETTER X

Join Bodhi in the classroom teaching the children the X breath. Breathing in through your nose as your draw the first part of a very big X, and breathe out through your nose as you draw the second part of the X.

You can start with small X's and make them bigger and bigger. How big can you get your X?

YAWNING

Take a big yawn and stretch your arms out. Breathe in and out through your mouth. Do two yawns after each other and sigh the breath out.

See how wide you can open your mouth when you yawn. Use your arms and stretch as you yawn and scrunch your face.

A yawn is a great way to stretch your whole body and face.

I CAN USE THESE BREATHS WHEN ...

I FEEL ANXIOUS
Calming Breath (p. 16)
Flower Breath (p. 22)
Giraffe Breath (p. 24)
Humming Bee Breath (p. 26)

I FEEL TIRED
Jabulani Breath (p. 30)
Lions Breath (p. 34)
Quick Breath (p. 44)

I NEED TO FOCUS AND CONCENTRATE
Dolphin Breath (p. 18)
Numbers Breath (p. 38)
Ocean Breath (p. 40)
Take 5 Breath (p. 50)

I AM FEELING SAD
Bunny Breath (p. 14)
Kindness Breath (p. 32)
Palm Breath (p. 42)
Rainbow Breath (p. 46)

I NEED TO FEEL BRAVE
Earth Breath (p. 20)
Vuvuzela Breath (p. 54)
Warrior Breath (p. 56)

BREATH IS MY SUPERPOWER.

ABOUT THE CONTRIBUTORS

Audrey Redmond is a qualified Physiotherapist and Breathwork Practitioner. She makes breathwork fun for kids through her creative play and embodiment practices. Her two children, Jonty and Sabi, offer assistance along the way. This fun way of learning helps children to feel their breath and to empower them with the knowledge of how to self-regulate.

Audrey's knowledge is grounded in the science of breath and her practical experience supports her teaching and ongoing research.

Marj Murray is a Certified Breathwork Practitioner and part of the Breathwork Africa team, having started the organisation with Dr Ela Manga in 2018. Marj loves working with children and finds that sharing breathwork with them supports focus, relaxation, and energy management, but most of all it is great fun!

Both Audrey and Marj strongly believe that conscious breathing is a life skill that should be shared within homes and taught in schools and all organisations across the globe. They hope that *The Alphabet Book of Breathing for Children* creates a greater awareness of this simple and effective tool that we all have right under our noses.

Brian van Wyk is an animator and draws pictures for a living, while skateboarding for a hobby. Brian not only had fun doing these illustrations but also learnt a lot about conscious breathing throughout the process.

www.ingramcontent.com/pod-product-compliance
Lightning Source LLC
Chambersburg PA
CBHW062043290426
44109CB00026B/2718